Adirondack Waters: Beneath the Surface

adult coloring book

Drawings to transport you to an aquatic world

Written and Illustrated by

Dave Campbell

inkminers.com - Saranac Lake, NY 12983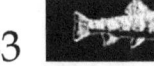

Adirondack Waters: Beneath the Surface

Coloring Book by Dave Campbell

Prepared, printed and bound in the USA

ISBN **978-0-9974393-1-1**

inkminers.com

47 Tara Drive

Saranac Lake, NY 12983

Writing, illustrations and cover design by Dave Campbell

Art Consultant: R. E. Brown

I have always been fascinated by what happens just under the surface of wild waters, where we get only a glimpse of the activity and seldom get to meet the residents face to face. I hope that you find some hours of peace, relaxation and artistic expression in these pages and allow this book to give you a break from the stresses of life. If it awakens memories of your favorite waters and shares just a bit of the magic from under the water's surface, it will have done its job.

ENJOY!

Dave

Table of Contents

By the way…...I lost a fishing lure in each of the pictures. See if you can find them!

Instructions:

I am often asked how to color that area where the surface of the water meets the air or areas in the distance under water. The simple answer is, "any way you please!" Just to give you some ideas, if you remember being a child, looking up through the water at friends on the surface, they were distorted by the motion of the water's surface. So was the view when standing above and looking into the water. The more clear the water and calm the surface, the less the distortion. Distance in water is far less clear than in the air. It quickly fades to a fuzzy, indistinct, and softly colored wall, so coloring those areas has many possibilities. The back cover may give you a few more ideas, but regardless of what you choose to do, you are always going to be right because it's your book, and each scene is yours. Play with them, and see what you like!

Crappies like the warmer Adirondack lakes and ponds, and their favorite hangout is fallen timber or sunken brush. They school up where food is abundant, and they prefer minnows but enjoy insects and small crustaceans as well. Fishermen frequently attract them by sinking bundled brush and evergreen trees six to ten feet deep. This cover attracts minnow and insect species looking for protection from predators, and the surfaces of the sticks provide an environment for algae growth which feeds many organisms. Those organisms serve as food for the small fish and crustaceans, so the brush pile becomes good habitat for a host of creatures, and that attracts the crappies

Crappies

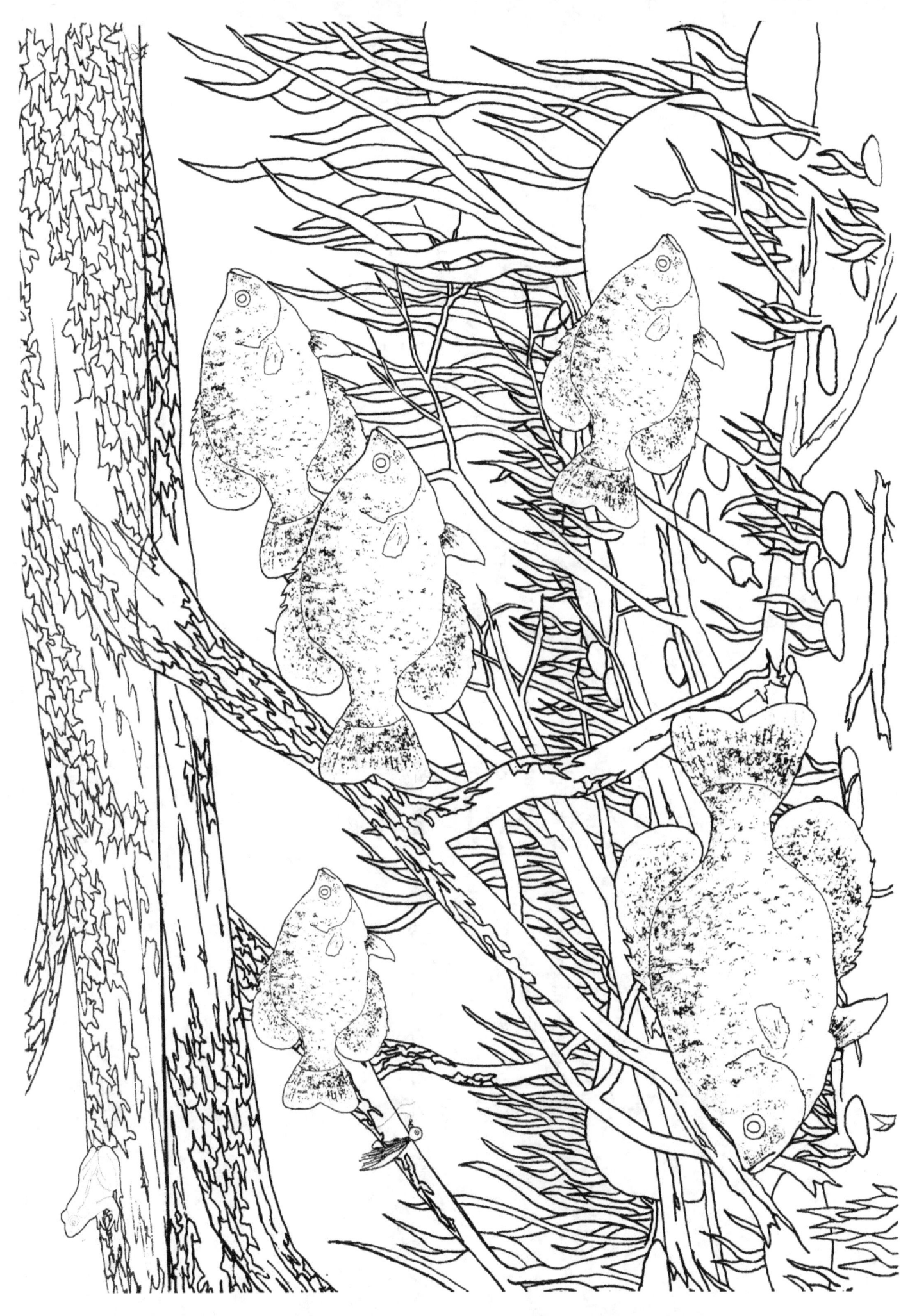

Chain Pickerel are not common, but they are found in the Adirondacks' warm ponds and larger lake shallows. Pickerel are well camouflaged with a green top and sides and a lighter whitish or yellowish chain-like pattern on their flank. An excellent example of a creature adapting to fit an environmental niche, they hide in shallow water cover so thick that people would be surprised anything could be in there. They dart out after frogs, minnows, small snakes, swimming mice, and even birds. Their mouth is lined top and bottom with razor sharp teeth, and fishermen quickly learn to avoid those teeth when unhooking a pickerel. Like their cousin, the northern pike, their long, thin profile makes them lightning fast when they strike.

Pickerel

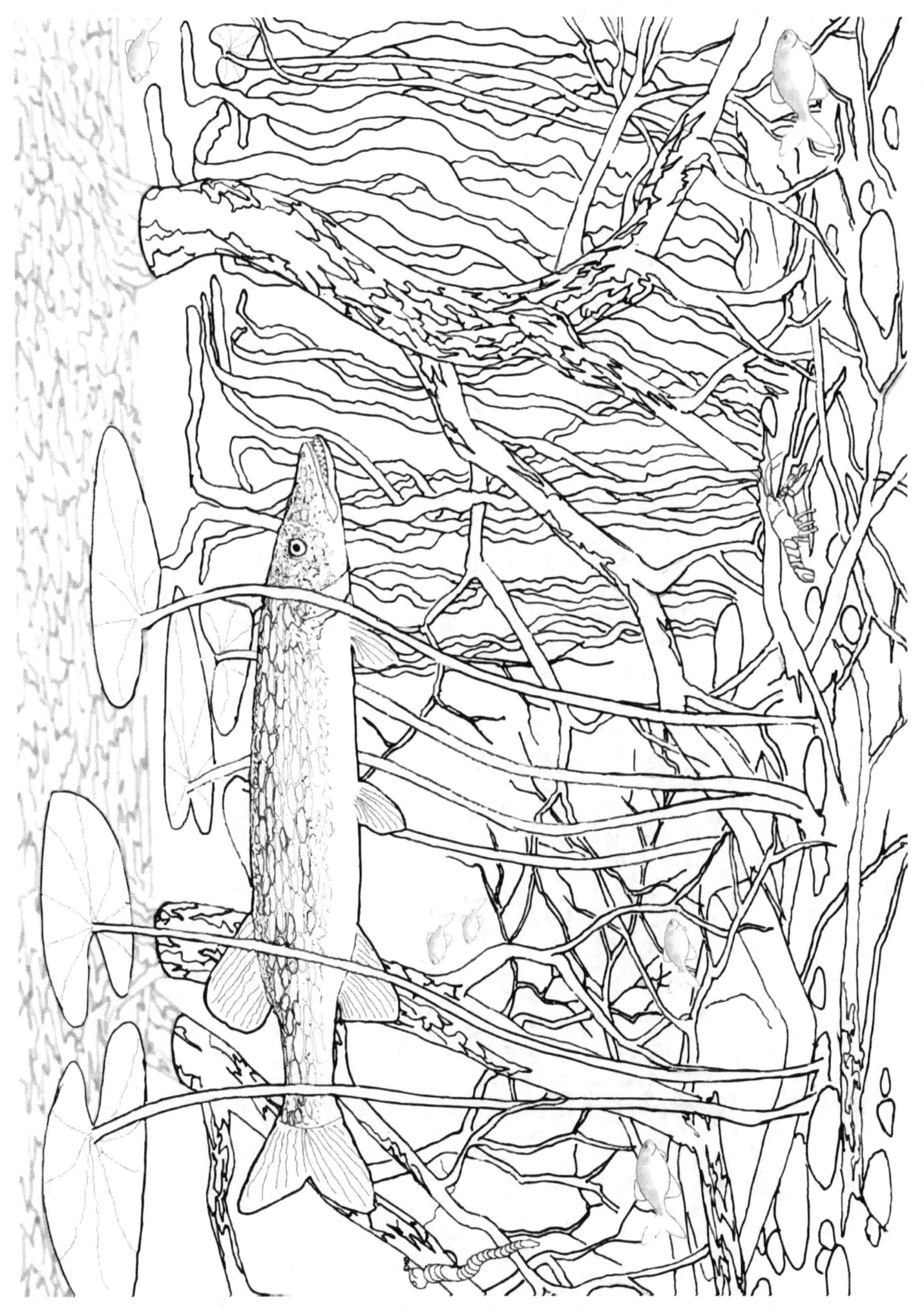

Bullheads may be the most common and widely distributed fish in Adirondack waters. They are members of the catfish family and can withstand warmer water and lower oxygen than other fish, so they are often the only residents in the boggier, warmer ponds where little else can survive. Although bullheads can grow to over two pounds, it is rare since they often overpopulate and stunt as a result. They eat both living and dead creatures, and they feed with the help of their "whiskers" which help them "taste" the waters around them. The sharp spine on the front of their dorsal fin and each pectoral fin can inflict a painful wound, and it helps protect the bullhead from larger fish.

Bullheads

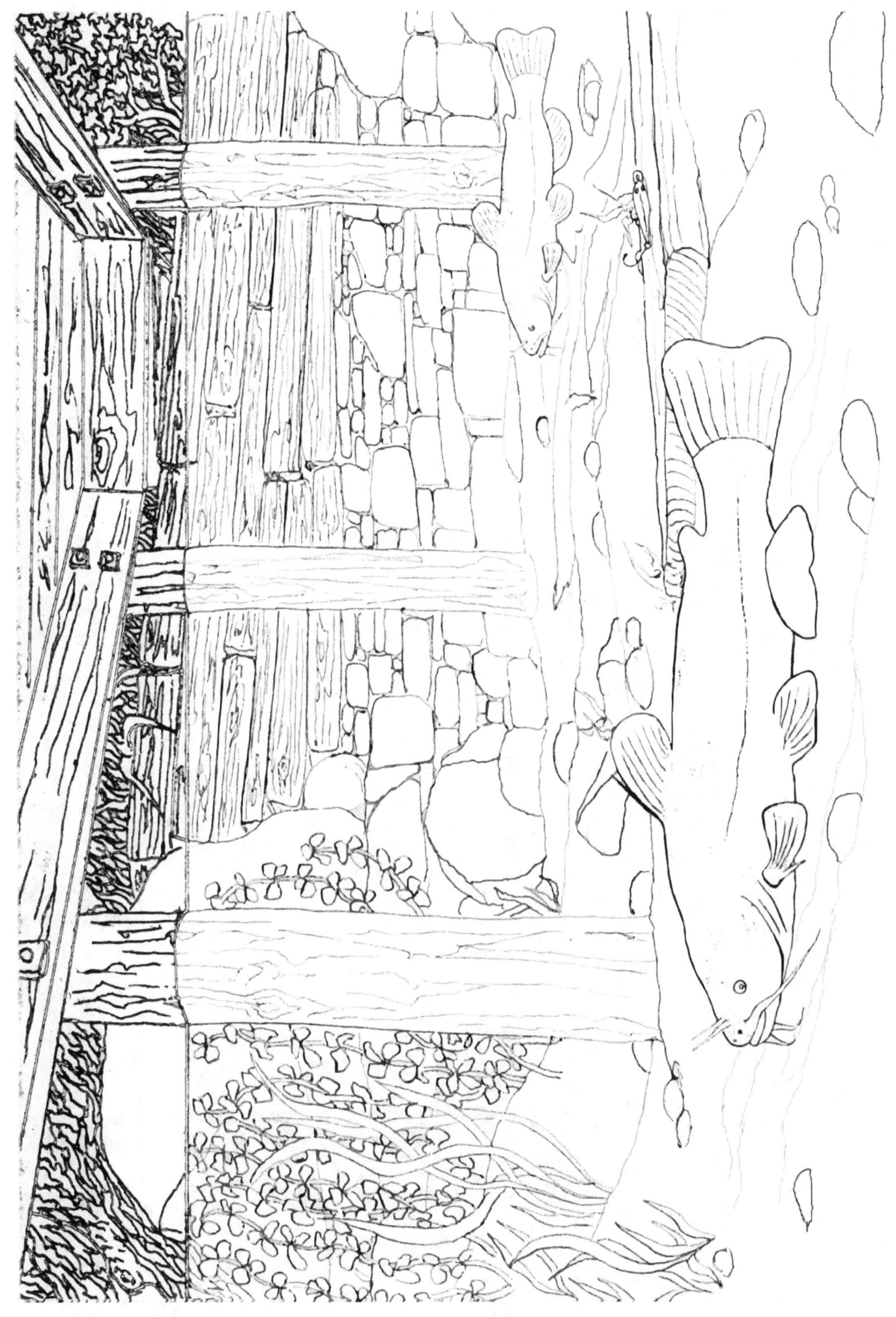

The smallmouth bass is a creature of both still and moving waters. Although closely related to the largemouth bass, smallmouths are more bronze colored, and the patterns on their sides match rippled sunlight on the underwater rocks where they are often found; an excellent example of camouflage through coloration. Smallmouths prefer rocky ledges and boulder strewn areas of ponds and lakes. In rivers or streams look for them in rocky areas and up against the undercut banks. They are aggressive, and they're called "smallmouth" only because their mouth is smaller than their "largemouth" cousins. If you draw a line straight down through a bass' eye, the hinge of the jaw on the smallmouth is forward of the line, and the largemouth's is to the rear of that line.

Smallmouths

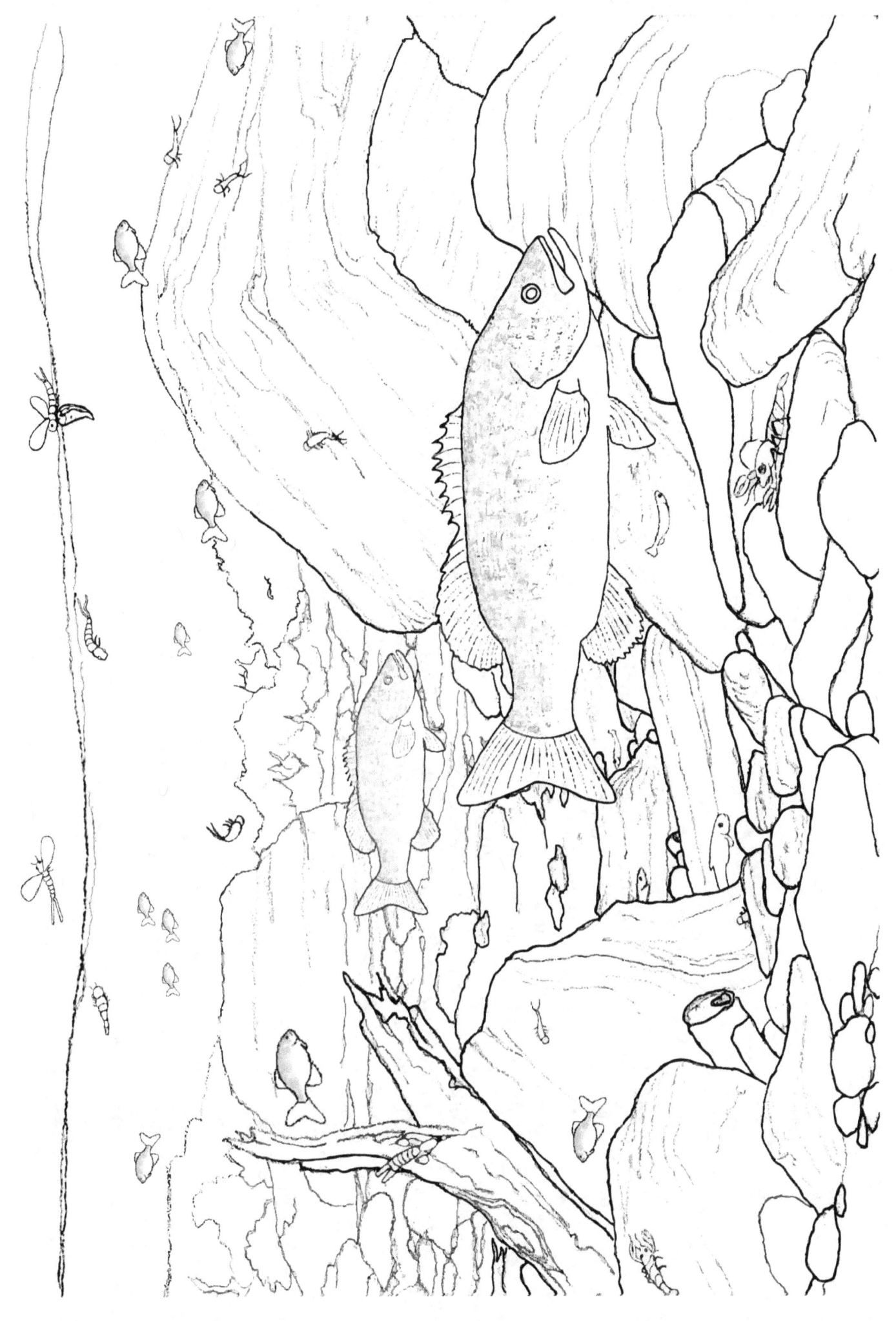

Rainbow trout are adaptable and live in both moving and still water. Rainbows, however, require cold water and ample oxygen. They are most often in deeper water in lakes or in faster moving stretches of streams where the water tumbles and churns, absorbing more oxygen. Rainbows also face less competition for food there since most other fish will choose slightly calmer, easier to navigate water. It's a great example of filling a niche in the environment. Originally native to areas west of the Rocky Mountains, rainbow trout were so popular among fishermen that they were stocked in waters all over the country, including the Adirondacks. They are now common here. They're called "rainbows" because of the distinctive pink stripe down their side.

Rainbows

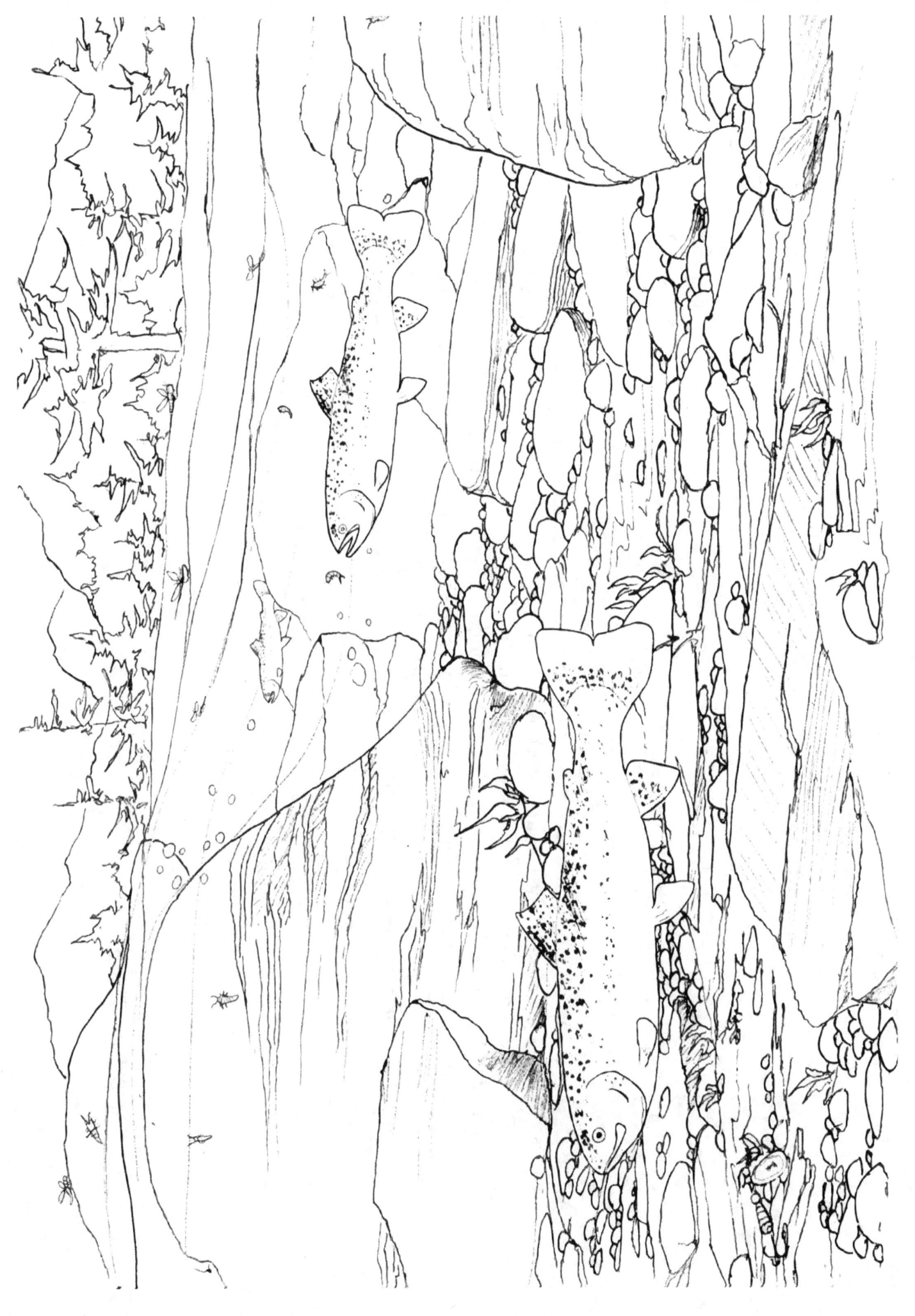

The largemouth bass is technically a member of the sunfish family. It is a very popular game fish found in both still waters and slow moving rivers in the Adirondacks. The largemouth's growth is limited by the Adirondacks' short growing season, but two to five pound fish are not uncommon. Unfortunately, they have been illegally introduced into trout waters, where they devastate trout populations. They will swallow almost anything that moves and fits in their mouth, which opens to almost the width of their body. Generally greenish, their coloration and markings depend on their surroundings, and murkier water results in a more brownish tint and less distinct markings. These fish love "cover" and are found around fallen timber, lily pads, weed beds, reeds and ledges. Largemouths feed on the bottom or the surface and everywhere between.

Largemouths

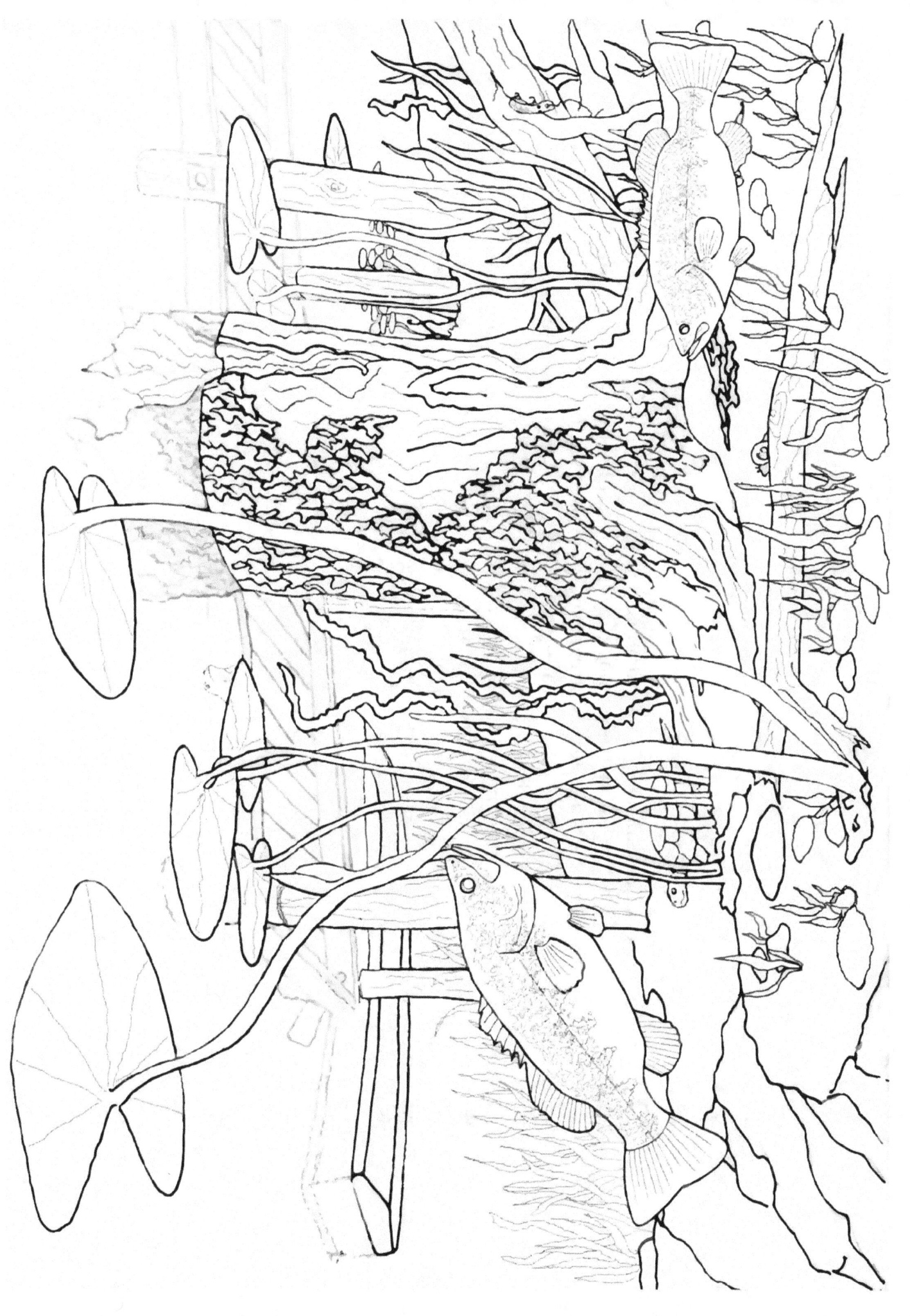

The remarkable American eel is "catadromous." Striped bass and Atlantic salmon are examples of "anadromous" fish, meaning they live as adults in large lakes or the ocean, and they run up rivers and feeder streams to spawn. Catadromous fish reverse that pattern, living in inland lakes and streams as adults but heading down to the ocean to spawn. Imagine the journey the eels make from the middle of the mountains, down streams and rivers, and out to the middle of the Atlantic to lay their eggs in the Sargasso Sea. The young, called "elvers," eventually make their way back to the streams and rivers and begin the cycle again. Unfortunately, dams have created barriers to eels returning from the sea. As a result of the damming, eels are neither as plentiful nor as widespread in the Adirondacks as they once were.

Eel

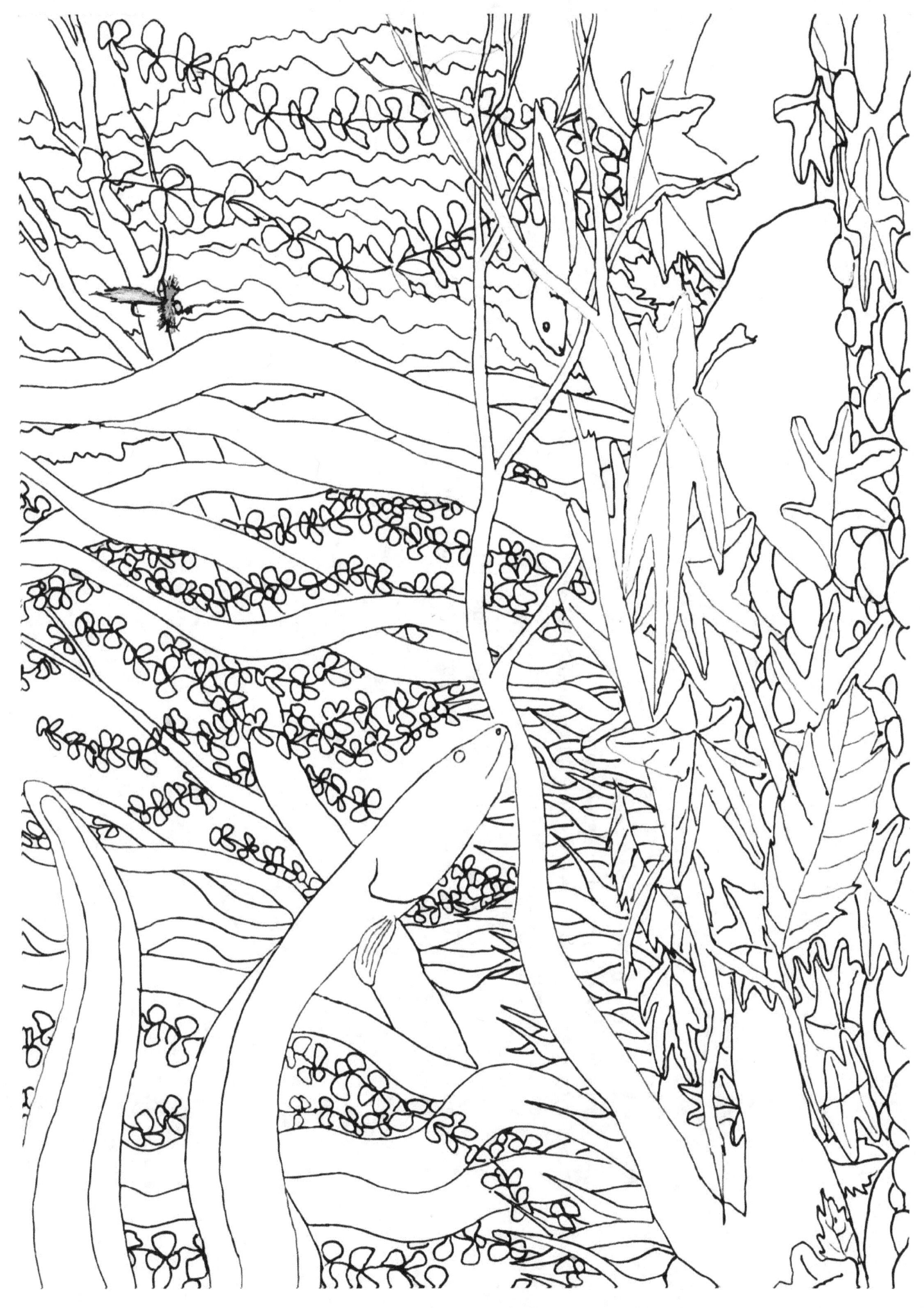

The northern pike is the most formidable predator in Adirondack waters. They are ambush hunters like their smaller pickerel cousins, so they prefer thick cover. Long and slender with indistinct green side markings and a darker back, pike seem to disappear against the weeds and fallen timber where they lurk. In rocky lakes and ponds pike hold in the shadows of ledges or between boulders, waiting for prey to come within range of their lightning fast strike. Pike grow quite large with fifteen to twenty pounds not being uncommon. Their razor sharp teeth ensure that nothing escapes their mouth, and they eat fish, frogs, snakes, and even small birds and ducklings. The frog in this scene is in deadly peril!

Pike

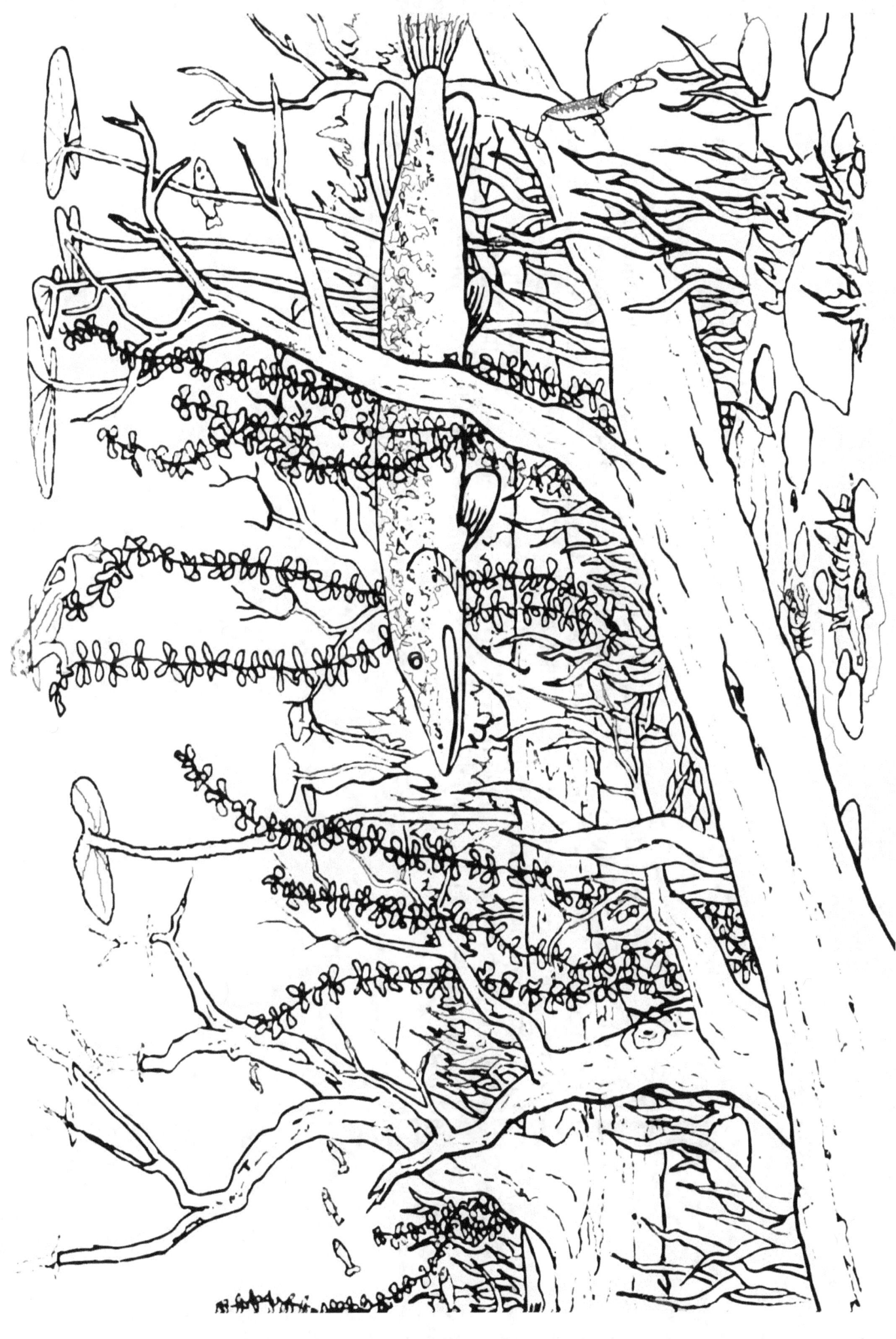

Rock bass are found in all kinds of water, from fast moving streams to still ponds. Rock bass have a relatively large mouth for their size and distinctive red eyes. Dining on small crustaceans, minnows and insects, rock bass are aggressive, often outrunning competing perch and sunfish when feeding. Only six to ten inches long when full grown, they are thick and strong like their largemouth and smallmouth cousins. Their golden brown to reddish brown color serves them well in the rocky habitat they prefer when it's available. When it's not, rock bass happily inhabit weeds or downed timber.

Rock Bass

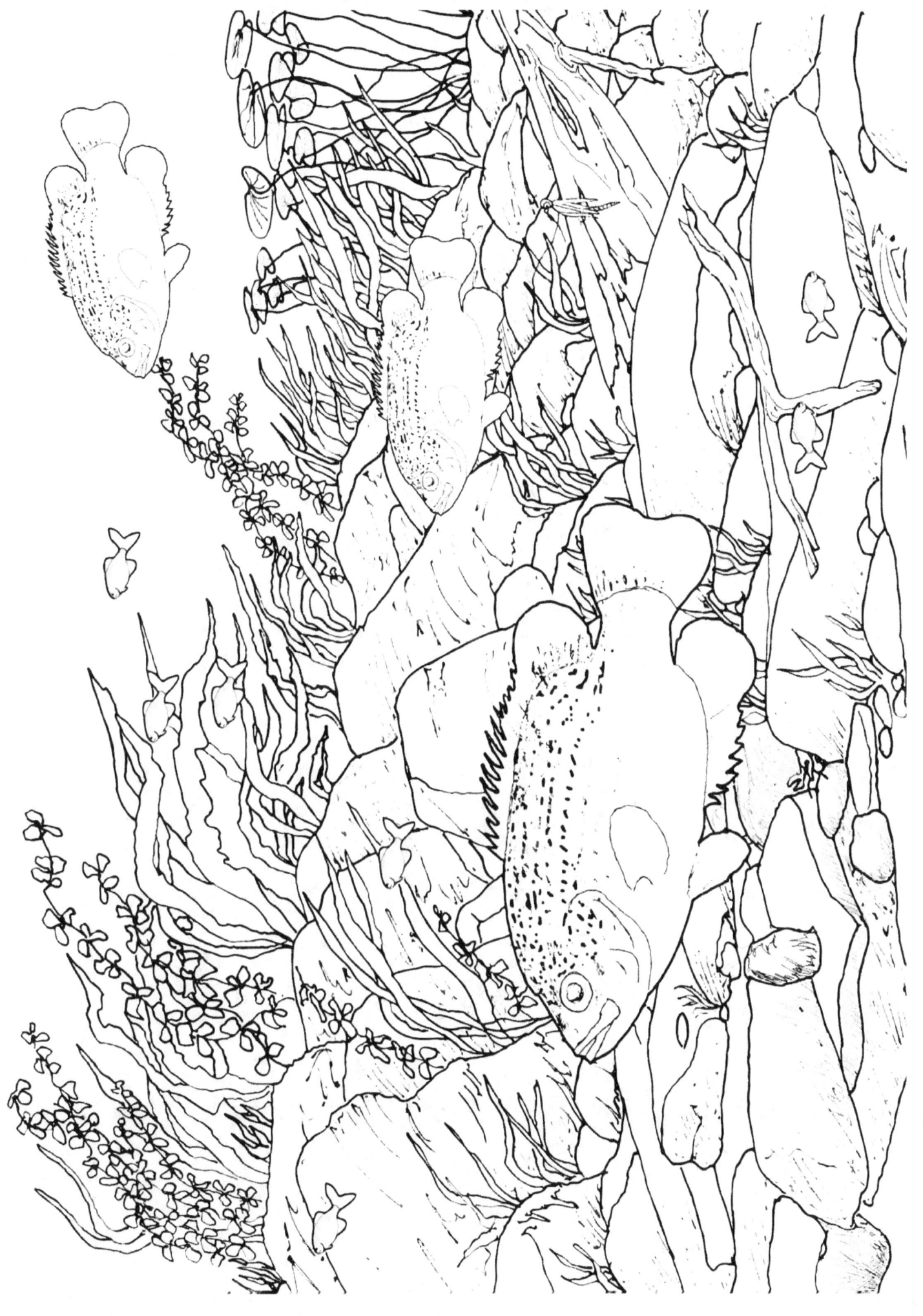

Shallows are teeming with life, with plenty of warming sunlight to stimulate plant and algae growth, providing food and cover for a host of creatures. The young of many insects, and most fish, reptile, amphibian, and crustacean species hide here as well. Young crawfish prey on insects and tiny young fish (called "fry"). The hellgrammite (larval form of the dobson fly) and dragon fly nymph are predators of other insects or small tadpoles and minnows. Some caddis fly nymphs excrete a silk-like substance to bond together bits of gravel, sand, and sticks to create a protective shell. Many of the creatures here feed on the plankton and algae growing on bottom debris and plant stalks. There is plenty of drama, and the shallows are a busy, fascinating, and dangerous place.

Shallows

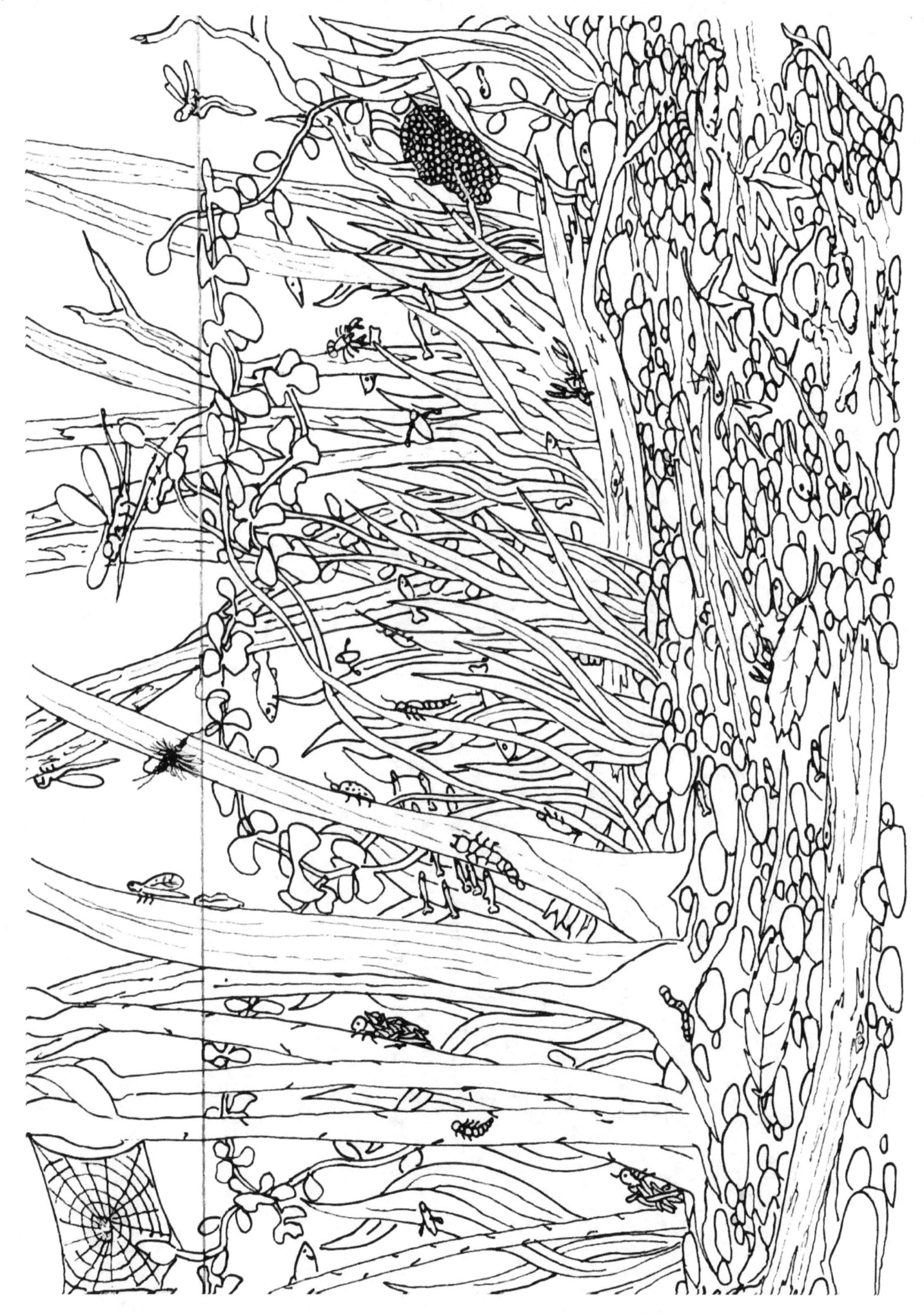

L
ake trout can grow up to forty pounds, and they can swallow a foot long sucker or even another trout. Being shy of sunlight, lakers prowl the rock crib pilings of Adirondack docks and the sandy shallows at night, looking for something to eat. Technically a member of the char family, the lake trout is closely related to the brook trout and sometimes interbreeds with them, creating a hybrid trout known as "splake" with some characteristics of each parent. Stand on a dock or boathouse deck on a summer night, and shine a flashlight down toward the bottom. You might glimpse one of these denizens looking for its next meal. Lakers live in the depths where little sunlight penetrates, so there is little camouflage needed. They have a dark green back, light green sides, and minimal "worm track" markings in dull white on their flanks.

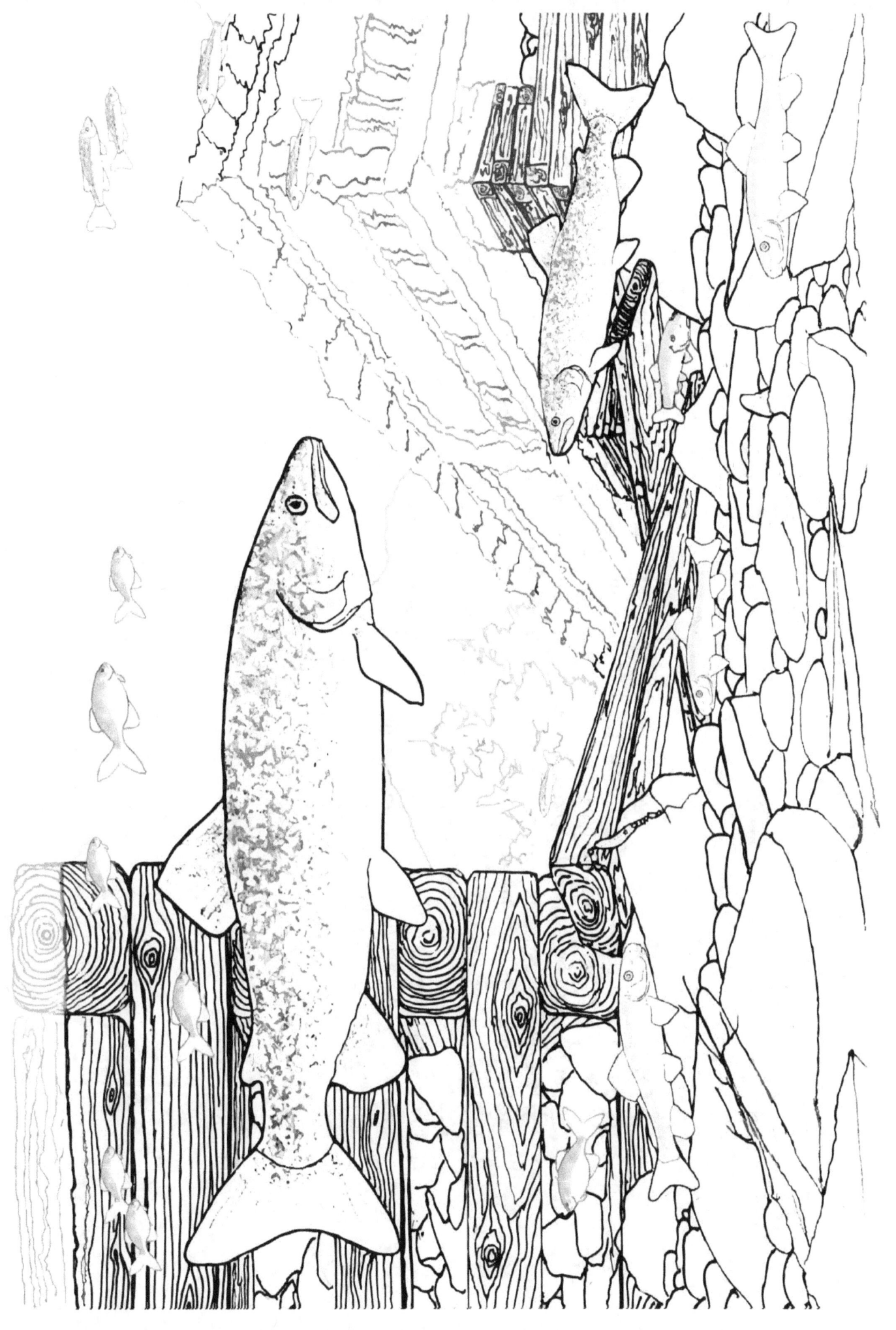

$\mathbf{M}$ost Adirondack waters have at least a few resident crawfish. Looking much like miniature lobsters, these freshwater crustaceans come in a variety of sizes. They can range from half an inch up to four inches long in good feeding areas. They catch live food, feast on dead creatures on the bottom, and snack on plant matter as well. Here, a dead minnow has attracted a number of crawfish, and battle may ensue for possession of the prize. They are primarily nocturnal. They hide under rocks and debris for their own safety since raccoons, herons, and many fish will actively hunt them. They can swim backwards with quick, strong strokes of their tail propelling them in spurts, but they prefer to walk forward on the bottom on their eight legs. They patrol their territory for food or invade a neighbor's if the scent of food attracts them.

Crawfish

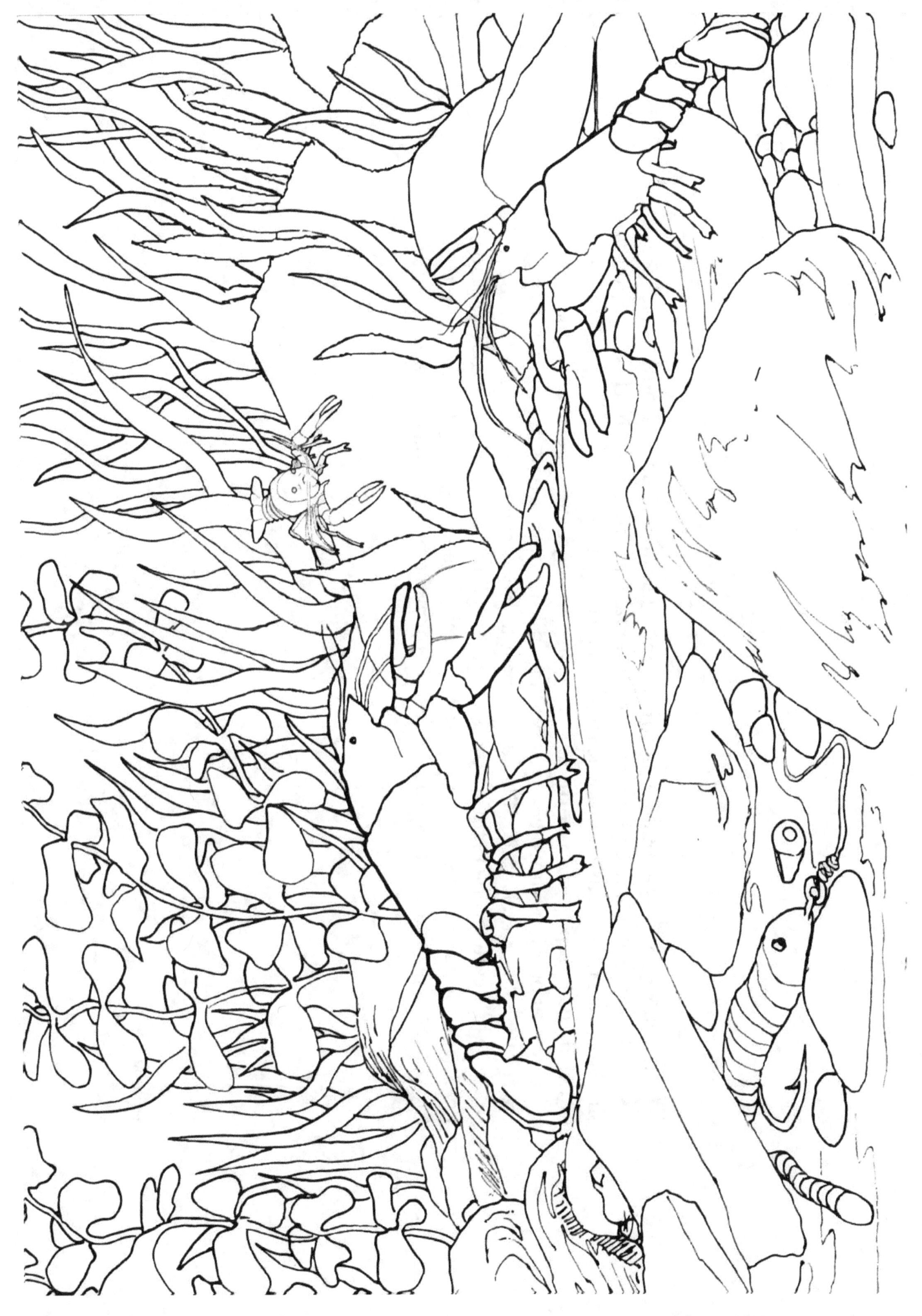

The yellow perch is another widespread and plentiful resident of Adirondack waters, and they seem comfortable in almost all aquatic habitats. Perch school in groups of similar sized fish to chase minnows, feed on hatching insect larvae, or scour the bottom or weed beds for prey of opportunity. They are an aggressive species, and the Department of Environmental Conservation will sometimes poison an entire pond to eradicate yellow perch and bullheads in order to create safer habitat for less competitive trout. While controversial, this process of "reclamation" has worked well for decades. Perch are popular targets all summer for fisherman, and they are often caught through the winter ice as well. Some people consider them the best tasting freshwater fish.

Yellow Perch

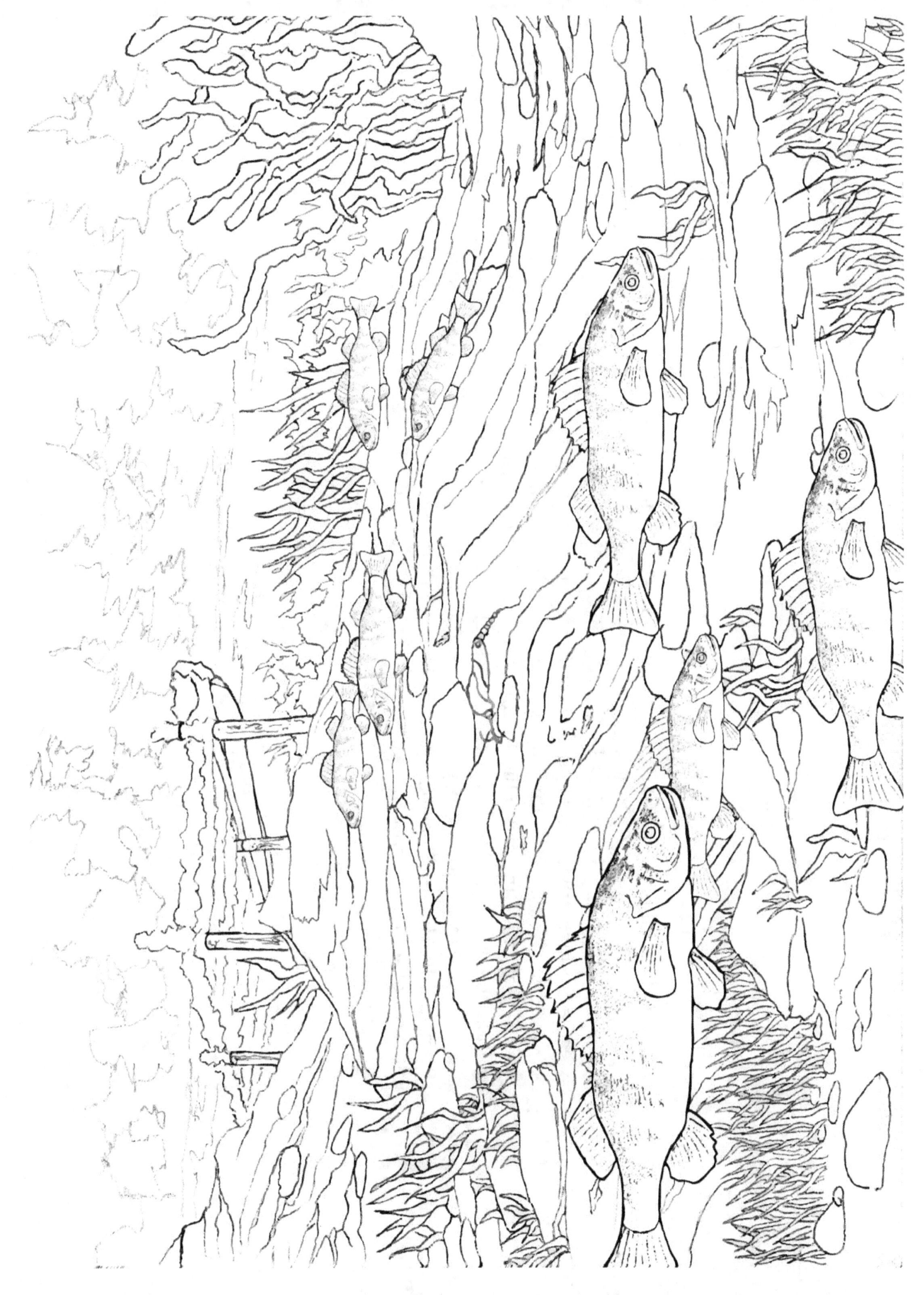

L andlocked salmon are fast, strong, and renowned for leaps and wild runs when hooked. A strain of Atlantic salmon living in waters that do not allow them access to the sea, they live their adult lives in lakes or ponds. They feed on forage fish, particularly smelt when available. Unfortunately, deforestation and resulting stream sedimentation in the last century destroyed the viability of many salmon spawning streams. Damming increased the sedimentation and reduced access to spawning grounds. Landlocked salmon fry require a sediment free gravel bottom with substantial stream flow to thrive for up to a year or more before venturing down to the lake to become adults. Populations have been maintained through hatchery production since little natural spawning now takes place. Landlocks are found in a few Adirondack ponds and lakes.

Landlocks

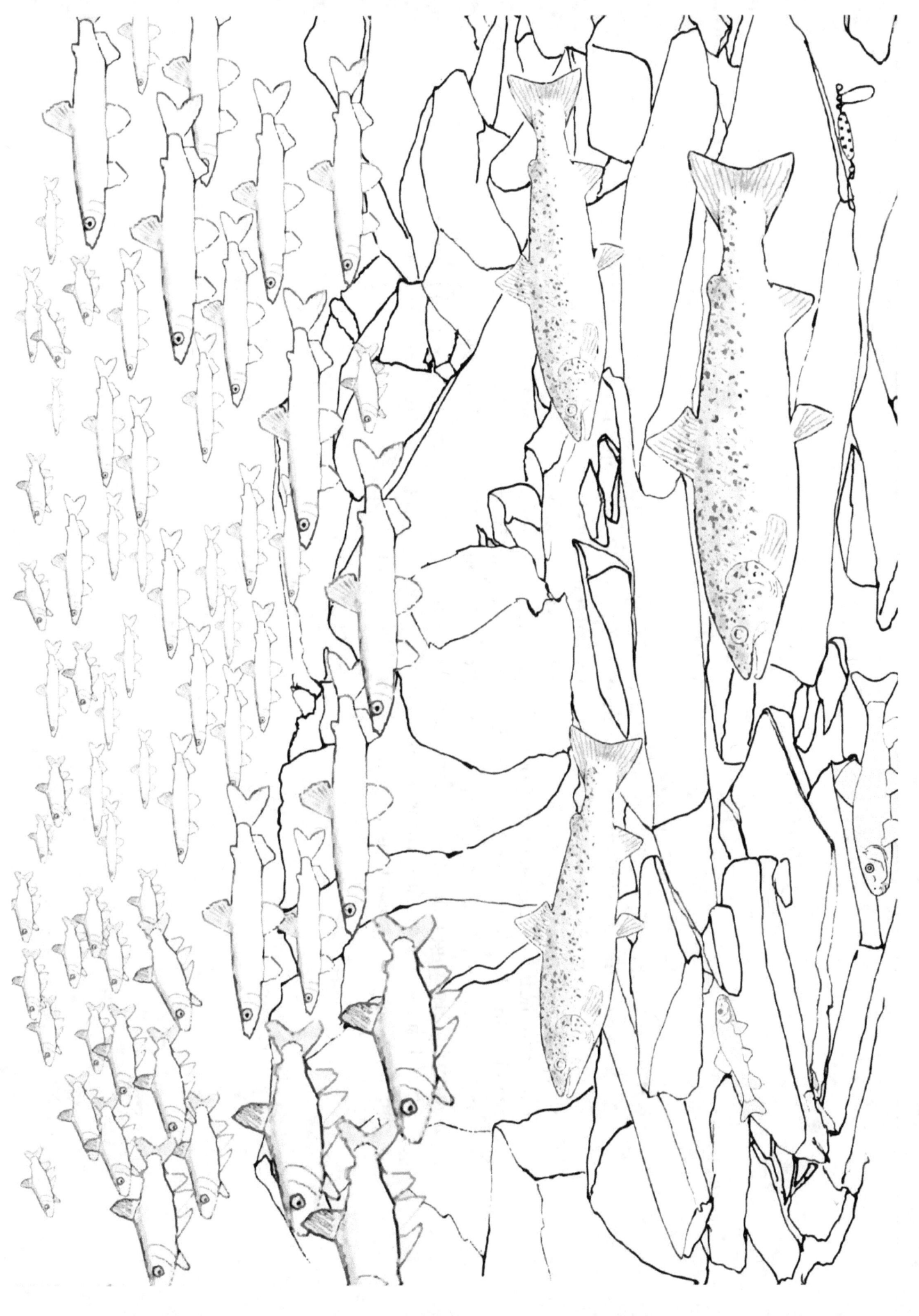

A variety of frog species entertain our children and startle us with quick escape leaps as we walk the shallows or shoreline. Frogs are not just prey for herons, bass, pike and other stream-side predators but are top-notch hunters themselves. They will eat insects, small snakes, mice, young birds, minnows, crawfish, and most anything else they can fit in their mouth, including other frogs. Each summer, watching young frogs develop inside jelly-like egg masses, become tiny algae eating tadpoles, and then grow legs while losing their tails is a fascination for children. Adult frogs' hind legs are surprisingly long when fully extended while swimming or leaping. Frogs spend winter buried in the mud or leaf litter on the bottom of lakes, ponds, and streams in a hibernative state, absorbing oxygen through their skin.

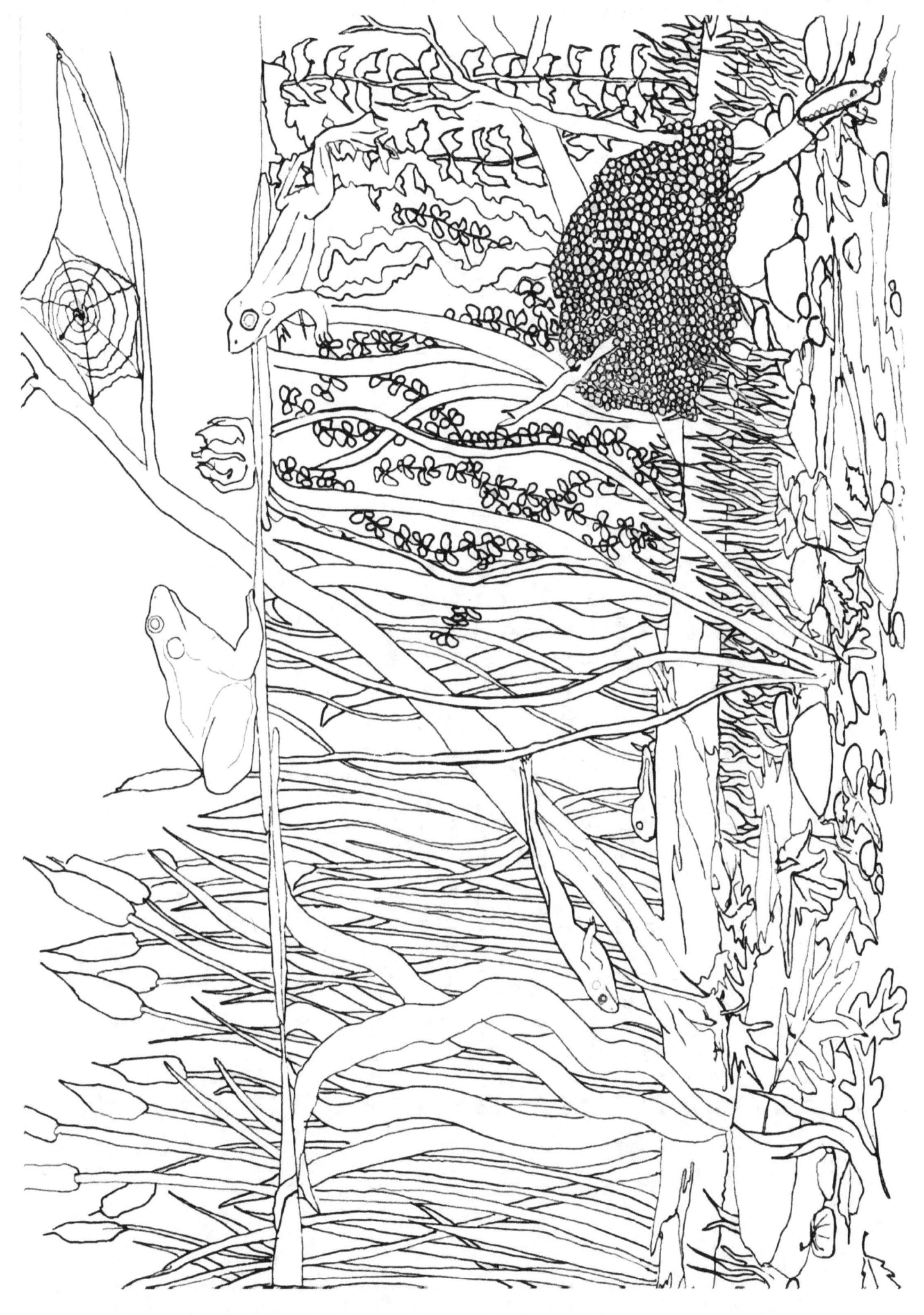

The term "Sunfish" is actually the name of a group of fishes, including largemouth and smallmouth bass. In common use, though, sunfish refers to those residents of most Adirondack waters that we see moving in and out of the weeds and brush in the sunlight. Pumpkinseeds are the most common species of sunfish, with beautifully iridescent blues and greens streaked across their cheeks and their "pumpkinseed" shaped bodies. Depending on which Adirondack water you visit, you may also find bluegills, redbreast, or longear sunfish. Sunfish are often the first fish children catch since the young sunnies aren't sophisticated and stay close to shore. They are food for many fish, birds and mammals. Larger sunfish like deeper water except at spawning time when they create crater-like depressions in the shallows with sand and gravel in which to lay and tend their eggs. They eat almost anything they can fit in their small mouths.

Sunfish

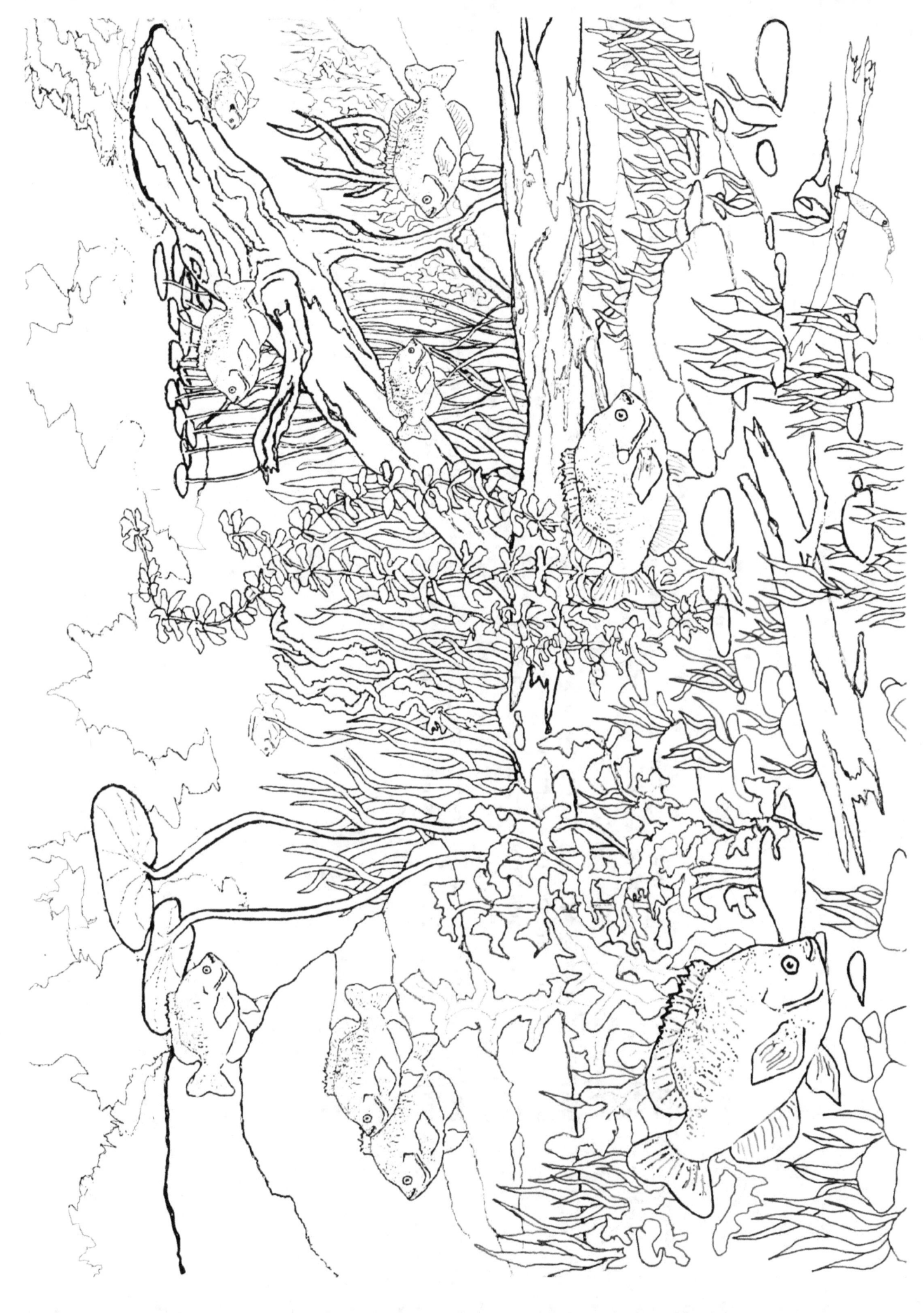

B rown Trout can withstand warmer temperatures and competition with other fish better than brook trout, and browns are becoming increasingly common in Adirondack waters. Originally imported from Germany, browns are beautifully colored with red and black spots, sometimes black ringed red spots, and a golden brown color. In streams, they are perfectly camouflaged for gravel bottoms and broken rocks, but in large lakes and ponds they become less colorful as they cruise open waters, preying on smelt, shiners, or other schooling minnows. Browns can grow very large in big lakes, feeding on insects, crawfish and minnows, and eventually adult fish of any species. They frequent undercut banks and sunken tree roots or scattered rocks in streams.

Browns

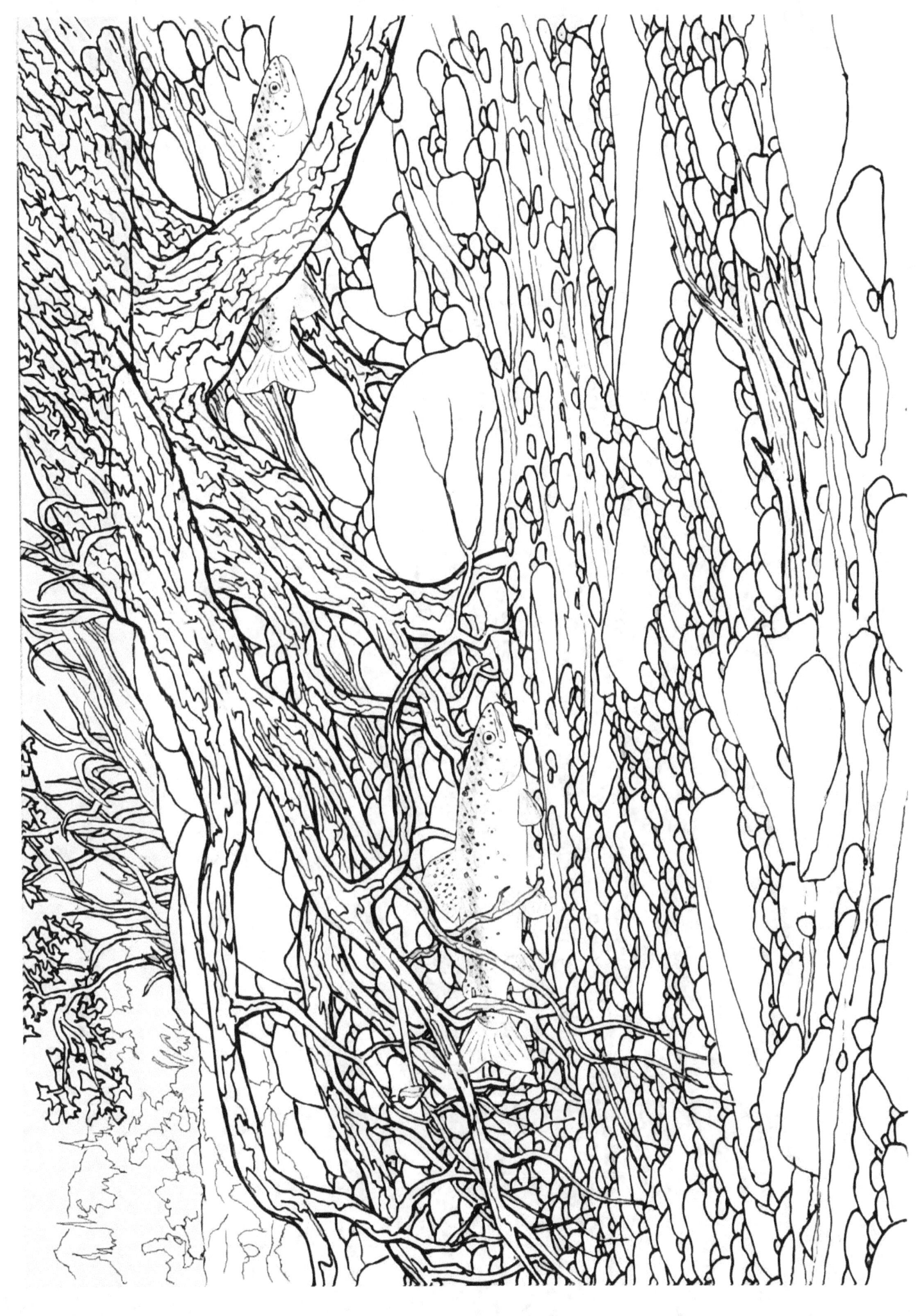

Rainbow Smelt, commonly known just as "smelt," are a forage fish in many lakes and ponds. They are also predators, feeding on fry and all sorts of small aquatic creatures. Preferring deep, cold waters, smelt usually form large schools know as "balls" that suspend in the middle of the lake or pond to avoid predators. Smelt run up small brooks to spawn, returning to the main lake afterwards, and they may spawn half a dozen times in their lifetime. Smelt are prized as a food fish and can be caught through the ice or scoop netted in streams while spawning. They are also used as bait. Because smelt prey on game fish fry, and eat the same food as young game fish, stocking them as food for adult game fish is not a simple decision for fisheries managers.

Smelt

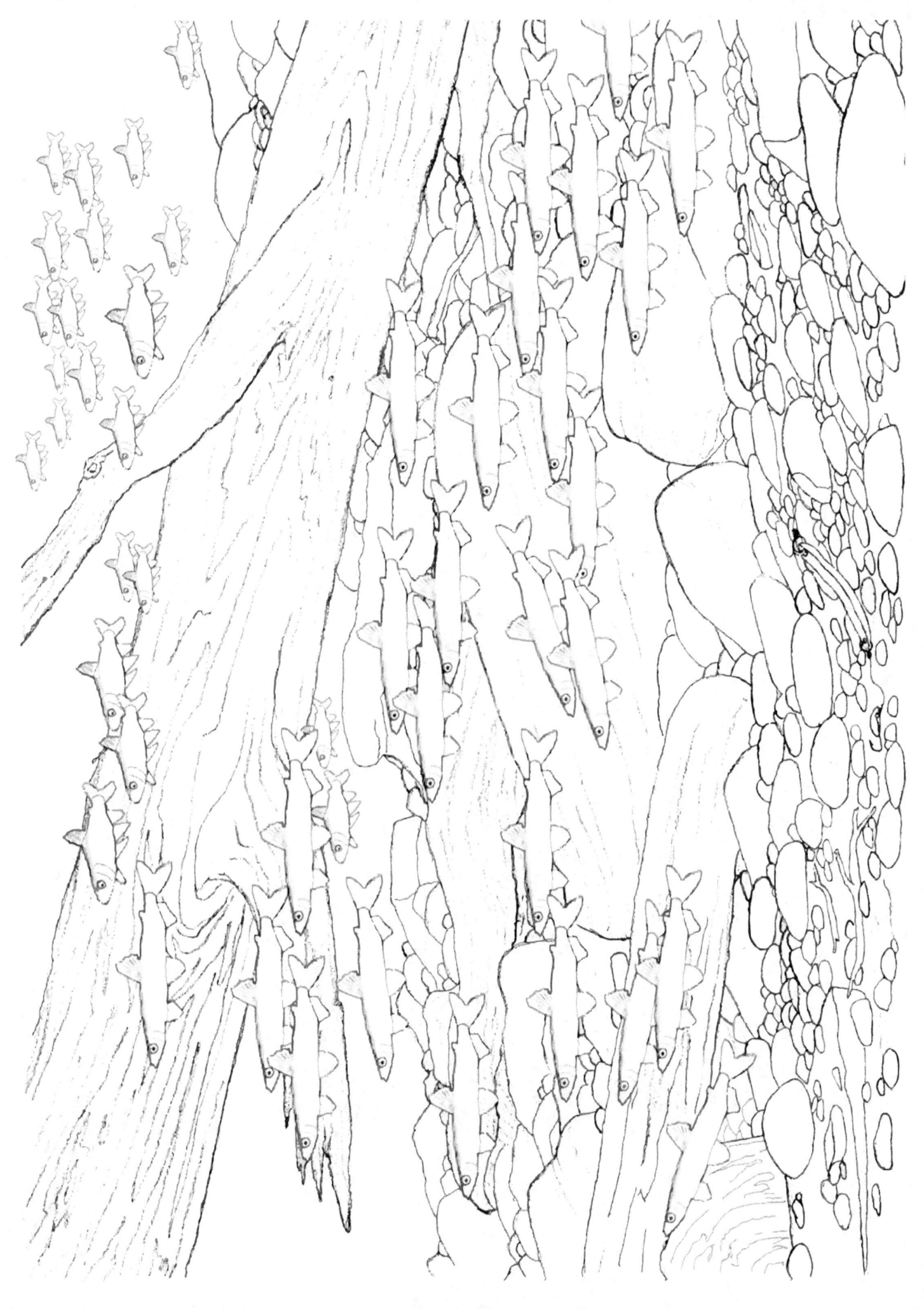

The quiet, unobtrusive painted turtle sunning on a log always makes me envious. Their bright yellow and orange markings make them a beautiful sight on a sunny day. The painted turtle reaches a length of only six to eight inches and is quite wary, disappearing underwater at the first approach of humans. The second turtle species native to the Adirondacks is the snapping turtle, an efficient predator that can reach seventy pounds although that's rare in the Adirondacks. Their hard edged, beak-like jaws can kill live prey, tear into carcasses, and easily damage a hand or finger. Approach with caution. The snapper's plain dark green or grey color camouflages it in the muddy, murky water it prefers.

Turtles

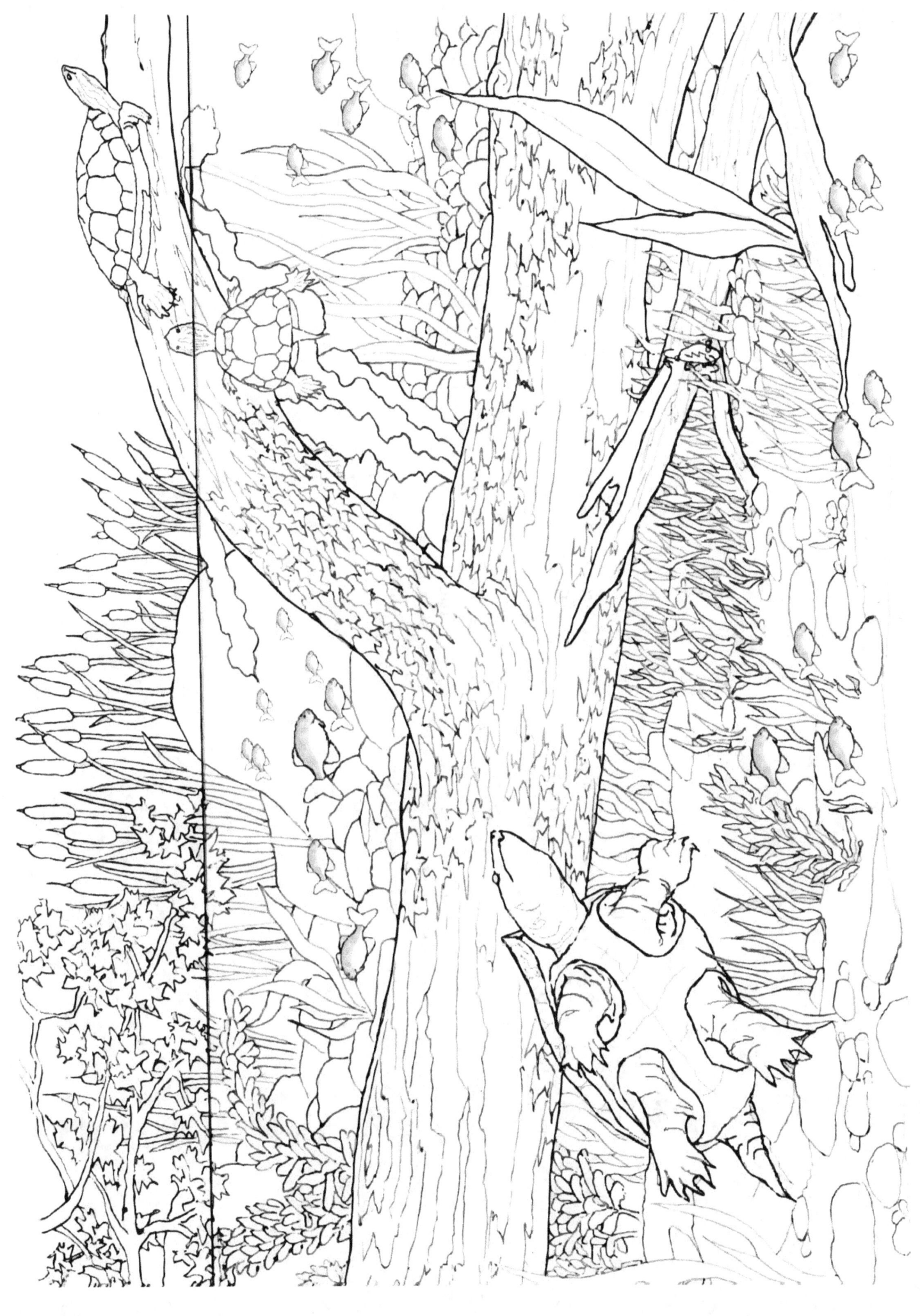

Brook trout are the signature fish of the Adirondacks, and they are versatile and adaptable while simultaneously fragile and limited. They inhabit large lakes, small ponds, rushing rivers, and tiny brooks. Mature brook trout can be very small while living in the tiny pools and riffles of a brook, yet they can reach five pounds in food rich ponds or lakes with cold water and limited competition. Unless cold waters can be maintained with few competing species, their populations will continue to decline. Some strains are already endangered from ever increasing fishing pressure, illegal introductions of competing species, and the warmer water temperatures of recent decades. A beautiful fish in their fall spawning colors, brookies will be there for our children to show their children only with our effort and care.

Brookies

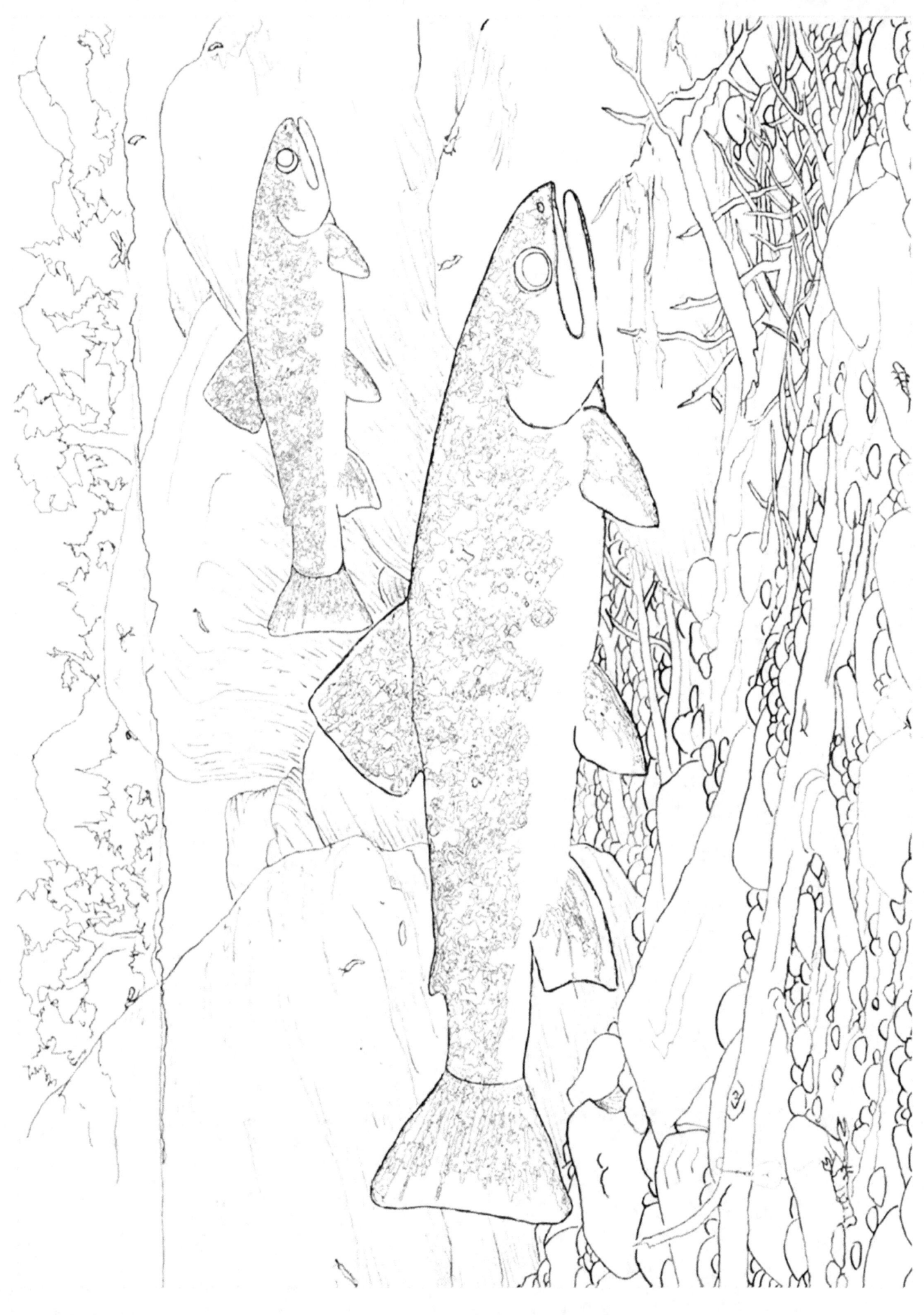

Thank you for joining me here! I hope you had a wonderful time under the surface. I also hope it has given you opportunities to escape the stresses of daily life and reclaim some time for "you." We all need to take more time for ourselves and provide some outlet for our artistic nature, be it large or small.

If you enjoyed this book, look for *The Adirondacks* adult coloring book, and *Beginners Guide to fishing.* You might enjoy them as well.

Dave

www.ingramcontent.com/pod-product-compliance
Lightning Source LLC
Chambersburg PA
CBHW080340290526
45791CB00009BA/2676